The Life of
Rupi Kaur

Exploring the Heart Behind
the Verses

Clayton J. Martin

Table of Contents

Chapter 1

Early Years

In the initial volume of our research into the life of Rupi Kaur, we delve into her formative years, learning the underlying aspects that would eventually transform her into the celebrated poet she is today. This part will explore her early life, her family history, and the cultural influences that had a key role in creating her personality and creativity.

Early Life:
Rupi Kaur was born on October 4, 1992, in Hoshiarpur, a small town in Punjab, India. Her birthplace, rich with cultural heritage and traditions, would have an unforgettable influence on her art and writing. Rupi was the youngest of three children, born to immigrant parents. Her family's journey is a quintessential immigrant narrative, one of

hopes and aspirations that transcended borders.

Rupi's parents, immigrants seeking better chances, settled in Canada when she was barely four years old. The immigrant experience played a vital role in molding her early impressions of the world. Adjusting to living in a new nation, coping with language obstacles, and adapting to a different culture provided Rupi with problems that would later be portrayed in her writing.

Family Background:
Rupi Kaur's family heritage is profoundly ingrained in Indian culture, and she grew up in a traditional Punjabi household. Her parents, who had relocated to Canada, established in her a strong attachment to her cultural heritage. The beliefs and traditions passed down from her parents would go on to impact her work and her devotion to social causes.

Rupi's family, like many immigrant families, placed a heavy priority on education. Her parents realized the importance of education in providing possibilities and a better life for their children. This focus on education became a driving factor in her early life, directing her toward a path of intellectual discovery and artistic expression.

Cultural Influences:
Growing up in a Punjabi household in Canada exposed Rupi to a combination of two unique cultures. She witnessed the rich tapestry of Indian traditions, from exciting festivals to wonderful cuisine, while also navigating the Western world. This dichotomy of cultural experience left a tremendous impact on her worldview and artistic sensibilities.

The cultural influences in Rupi Kaur's life stretched beyond her family. The broad and multicultural metropolis of Toronto, where she was raised, afforded her exposure to a wide spectrum of people and experiences. This pluralism expanded her perspective and played a vital role in molding her work, notably her later essays on identity and diversity.

Childhood Experiences:
Rupi Kaur's childhood was distinguished by both the difficulty of assimilation into a new culture and the delights of a close-knit family. Her early experiences were essential in cultivating her enthusiasm for art and expressiveness. As a child, she often found peace in her artistic interests, which served as an outlet for her ideas and emotions.

Her early exposure to art and creativity can be traced to the supportive atmosphere provided by her family. Encouraged by her parents, she began sketching and writing at a young age. These creative activities provided a tool for her to make sense of her reality and share her feelings.

Development of a Love for Art and Expression:

Rupi Kaur's affinity for art and expression blossomed as she improved her skills during her formative years. From sketching her thoughts in the margins of her school notebooks to authoring her first poems, she found in art a medium to articulate her thoughts and feelings.

The artistic environment in her household, with her mother's enthusiasm for sewing and her father's love for photography, further encouraged her creative talents. These early influences laid the seeds for Rupi's future endeavors as a poet and artist.

Rupi Kaur's early years were a combination of cultural richness, family values, and artistic discovery. Her upbringing in a Punjabi immigrant family, mixed with the cosmopolitan climate of Toronto, offered a healthy foundation for her to develop her love for art and expression. These early experiences created the groundwork for her later literary and artistic triumphs, which we shall explore further in the following chapters.

Chapter 2

Emigration to Canada

In this chapter, we look into the important decision of Rupi Kaur's family to relocate from India to Canada and the significant influence this transition had on her life. We also discuss the obstacles and adaptations they encountered as immigrants, as well as the dramatic cultural gap between their Indian background and their new Canadian home.

The decision to travel from their motherland of India to Canada was a key turning point in Rupi Kaur's family's lives. It was a decision prompted by the desire for greater possibilities, economic stability, and a brighter future for their children. Rupi's parents, like many others, went on this journey with ambitions and aspirations of providing their family with a better life.

The process of emigration was not without its hurdles. It meant negotiating bureaucratic difficulties, getting permits, and making the painful decision to leave behind their extended family and the familiarity of their hometown. Rupi's family was not uncommon in this regard, since millions of immigrants around the world make similar sacrifices and choices in quest of a better life.

Challenges Faced as Immigrants
Upon settling in Canada, Rupi Kaur's family experienced a number of obstacles that are similar to many immigrant families. Language problems were a considerable impediment, particularly for the elderly population. Rupi's parents had to adapt to a new language, English, while striving to preserve their native Punjabi and keep their cultural identity.

The procedure of seeking permanent employment in a new nation was another hurdle. Rupi's parents had to navigate the Canadian employment market, which typically needs skills and certifications that may not immediately transfer from one country to another. This period of transition was distinguished by hard labor, resilience, and the desire to provide a better life for their children.

Cultural Contrast

The cultural gap between India and Canada was clear and powerful. India, with its rich history, traditions, and close-knit communities, presented a dramatic contrast to the varied and diversified terrain of Canada. For Rupi, growing up in Canada meant negotiating a culture that was significantly more autonomous and less bound by traditional beliefs.

The change from a collectivist society to one that promotes individualism and personal autonomy brought about a cultural transformation for Rupi and her family. They had to adapt to a society where individual expression and individuality were encouraged, which would later impact Rupi's investigation of identity and feminism in her poems.

In this new cultural landscape, Rupi's family attempted to keep their Indian customs while simultaneously embracing Canadian ideals. This duality of cultural influences would become a key motif in Rupi's later work, representing the interplay between her Indian ancestry and her Canadian upbringing.

Adaptation and Assimilation

Despite the obstacles and cultural discrepancies, Rupi Kaur's family gradually acclimated to their new life in Canada. The children, particularly Rupi, assimilated more swiftly and fluidly, often serving as cultural intermediates between their parents and the Canadian environment. Education played a significant role in their adaptation since it gave possibilities for integration and personal growth.

The family's dedication, hard work, and commitment to their cultural heritage would shape Rupi's identity and artistic expression. Her unique perspective as an immigrant, with one foot in her ancestral culture and the other in her chosen land, would later be a driving force in her poetry, promoting themes of cultural identification and diversity.

The relocation of Rupi Kaur's family from India to Canada was a significant decision that transformed their lives and created the groundwork for Rupi's journey as a poet.

The struggles and adaptations they faced as immigrants, together with the cultural mismatch between their Indian background and Canadian surroundings, played a crucial influence in forming her worldview and artistic sensibilities. These experiences provide the backdrop against which Rupi Kaur's life and poems will eventually unfold.

Chapter 3

<u>Education and Early Creative Pursuits</u>

Rupi Kaur's educational experience in Canada began as she entered the Canadian school system as a young immigrant. Education was a primary focus in her household, and her parents had high aspirations for their children's academic achievement. Rupi's early years were distinguished by the obstacles of transitioning to a new education system and the linguistic gaps between Punjabi and English.

As a student, Rupi exhibited an early affinity for language and literature, which her professors appreciated. Despite the initial language barrier, her passion for studying and the support of her educators helped her to make tremendous progress in her schooling. She immediately became proficient in English, which played a vital part in her destiny as a writer.

The Influence of Educational Experiences

Rupi Kaur's formative years in the Canadian education system played a key part in her development as a writer. Her exposure to books and language in the Canadian classroom sparked her love for words and narrative. It was during these years that she began to understand the power of words as a form of expression and communication.

Early in her school career, Rupi found herself leaning toward the world of poetry and narrative. The structured, yet emotionally evocative quality of poetry connected with her, and she began experimenting with her own verses. Her tutors supported her emerging talent and provided instruction that would be important in her later writing career.

Writing as a Means of Expression

Writing became a tool for Rupi to communicate her thoughts and emotions. As a teenager, she started maintaining diaries in which she would scribble down her feelings, experiences, and observations. These writings served as a source of self-reflection and catharsis, allowing her to traverse the complexity of puberty and the obstacles of cultural identification.

Through her writing, Rupi tackled the topics of identity, belonging, and the immigrant experience. Her poems became a personal outlet for her feelings, and she found solace in her ability to put her ideas into words. This early dabbling with poetry laid the framework for her career as a poet and author.

Influential Teachers and Mentors

Throughout her school path, Rupi was fortunate to have supportive instructors and mentors who noticed her skill and pushed her to pursue her passion for writing. These educators sensed in Rupi the potential to become a skilled writer and nourished her love for reading.

The direction and encouragement she obtained from these prominent personalities equipped her with the confidence to continue writing and exploring her lyrical abilities. Their support was crucial in shaping her early creative activities and instilling in her the notion that her words possessed power and meaning.

The Transition to Higher Education

Rupi's scholastic path extended to higher school when she attended the University of Waterloo in Ontario. There, she pursued a degree in rhetoric and professional writing, a choice that coincided with her enthusiasm for words and stories. Her undergraduate experience further refined her writing talents and introduced her to a broader literary environment.

As a university student, Rupi continued to explore poetry and began sharing her work with a wider audience. She engaged in open mics, poetry readings, and creative writing workshops, where she met a supportive network of kindred writers and artists. These experiences contributed to the maturation of her poetic style and the development of her unique voice.

The Influence of Education on Her Poetry

Rupi Kaur's educational experiences, from her early years in the Canadian school system to her university degrees, left an indelible effect on her poems. The structure, discipline, and creativity she encountered in the classroom became crucial to her approach to writing.

The themes of cultural identification, language, and the immigrant experience that she examined in her early writings continued to resound in her poems. Her scholastic experience equipped her with the ability to compose verses that were not only emotionally resonant but also technically proficient. The mix between ordered form and genuine emotion became a characteristic of her work.

Rupi Kaur's scholastic path had a key influence on her development as a writer and poet. The support of her professors, the effect of her school experiences, and her investigation of literature and language all contributed to her early creative interests. These formative years created the framework for her emergence as a notable poet and the unique voice that would fascinate readers around the world.

Chapter 4

The Birth of an Artist

The genesis of Rupi Kaur's poetry can be traced back to her formative years, where her love for language and storytelling was developed via her educational experiences. As she transferred to further school at the University of Waterloo, her enthusiasm for writing began to express more strongly in the form of poetry.

Rupi's poetry generally draws from her personal experiences, feelings, and observations. She found inspiration in the intricacies of life, including love, relationships, identity, and the immigrant experience. Her early poetry was a manner of self-expression and a technique to analyze her own thoughts and feelings.

The writing process was highly personal for Rupi. She typically characterizes it as a therapeutic and transforming journey. Her writings were produced from reflection and a genuine connection to the human experience. The language she chose was simple yet profound, and it resonated with readers who found consolation and connection in her words.

Early Attempts at Sharing Her Work
Rupi Kaur's desire to share her poems with a wider audience led her to participate in open mics and poetry readings during her undergraduate years. These live performances allowed her to gauge the reactions of her audience and hone her literary style. It was during these events that she began to establish a following and receive positive feedback from those who enjoyed her work.

In 2013, Rupi Kaur made a key decision that would influence the path of her artistic life.

She created an Instagram account, @rupikaur_, and started sharing her poems and illustrations with the world. The website allowed her a unique opportunity to present her art and connect with a global audience.

The Impact of Social Media

Social media, and Instagram in particular, played a transforming impact in Rupi Kaur's early artistic pursuits. The platform allowed her to express her poetry in a visually attractive way, often merging her lines with her own illustrations. This multimedia technique brought an additional layer of significance to her work, making it more accessible and interesting for her following.

Rupi's poems connected with a varied audience, and her Instagram account swiftly acquired followers who enjoyed the relatability and genuineness of her work. Her posts went viral, and she began receiving letters from people who felt a great connection to her poems. This direct response from her audience was important in driving her creative desire.

One of the primary characteristics of Rupi Kaur's writing that attracted readers was her sensitivity and genuineness. She was unafraid to examine the raw and often unpleasant aspects of the human experience, such as suffering, heartbreak, self-discovery, and healing. Her willingness to express her own path and emotions made her poems approachable and reassuring to many who were going through similar circumstances.

Rupi's poems typically touched on common issues that resonated with individuals of many backgrounds, which contributed to the broad appeal of her work. Her verses were marked by brevity, clarity, and emotional depth, making them accessible to a wide spectrum of readers.

Empowerment Through Words

Rupi Kaur's early attempts at sharing her work were grounded by a desire to empower her readers. She utilized her poetry as a tool to inspire and uplift, particularly in the context of her investigation of feminism and the female experience. Her writings typically expressed lessons of strength, self-acceptance, and tenacity, which struck a chord with many women.

The global accessibility of social media allowed her thoughts to transcend regional boundaries and connect with folks from all cultures and backgrounds.

Rupi's work became a source of solace and empowerment for many who felt unheard or marginalized, and it generated discussions on significant societal issues.

The Viral Success of "Milk and Honey"

In 2014, Rupi Kaur's first novel, "Milk and Honey," was published. The book was a compilation of her poems and paintings, and it displayed her individual style and theme inquiry. "Milk and Honey" was a departure from standard poetry collections, since it mixed visual components with rhyme to create a new and engaging reading experience.

The book was first self-published and sold primarily through Rupi's Instagram account. Its success was, in part, due to the massive following she had developed on social media. Readers who had been following her on Instagram immediately embraced the opportunity to buy a physical copy of her work.

"Milk and Honey" immediately acquired popularity and became a bestseller, reaching readers throughout the world. Its impact was enormous, and it resonated particularly with a youthful and diverse audience. The book's themes of love, pain, healing, and self-discovery struck a chord with readers who saw their own experiences reflected in its pages.

Critics and researchers also took notice of "Milk and Honey," studying its structure, content, and the influence of social media on modern poetry. The book's success led to conversations about the shifting face of literature in the digital age and the potential of platforms like Instagram to elevate the voices of budding artists.

The genesis of Rupi Kaur's poetry and her early attempts at disseminating her work was intimately related to her personal experiences and her acceptance of social media. The strong combination of her sensitivity, genuineness, and relatability enables her poetry to connect with a varied global audience.

This chapter has covered the transforming impact of social media on her artistic path and the viral popularity of her first book, "Milk and Honey." Rupi Kaur's distinctive approach to storytelling and self-expression would pave the way for her rise as a notable poet and artist.

Chapter 5

Milk and Honey - A Literary Phenomenon

"Milk and Honey" symbolizes a crucial milestone in Rupi Kaur's literary path. The book, a compilation of poems and images, was born from her experiences, emotions, and the creative energy she cultivated through her early years. Rupi's choice to collect her work into a book was both a personal and professional turning point.

As Rupi continued to share her poetry on social media, she received an outpouring of enthusiastic feedback from her followers. Readers recognized their great connection to her words, often explaining how her poetry had helped them traverse their own feelings and experiences. Encouraged by this reception, Rupi wanted to combine her poems and images into a cohesive book that would offer a more immersive reading experience.

The process of selecting and compiling the poetry for "Milk and Honey" was profoundly personal for Rupi. It was a reflection of her personal journey, from grief to healing, and from self-discovery to empowerment. The book was organized into four sections, each depicting a particular phase of her life and the emotions that accompanied it. This theme structure gave the book a narrative quality, allowing readers to embark on a journey of their own as they dug into its pages.

Self-Publishing and Initial Distribution

Rupi Kaur elected to self-publish "Milk and Honey," a decision that would prove to be important in the book's popularity. Self-publishing offered her creative control over every aspect of the book, from its content to its graphic presentation. This allowed her to keep the sincerity and creative integrity that had resonated with her internet audience.

Rupi made "Milk and Honey" available for purchase on her own website and social media sites, including Instagram. The book's distribution was originally modest, as she did not have the backing of a regular publisher or an experienced literary agent. However, this grassroots approach to marketing and distribution afforded her direct contact with her fans and allowed her to retain a personal connection with her audience.

The Reception of "Milk and Honey"
The reception of "Milk and Honey" was nothing short of spectacular. As readers throughout the world discovered the book, they were intrigued by its real and accessible material. The themes of love, pain, healing, and self-discovery, presented in Rupi's

distinctive style, resonated deeply with a diverse audience.

Readers found consolation and connection in Rupi's poetry. Many thought that her words expressed emotions and experiences they had a hard to describing themselves. The simplicity and clarity of her rhymes, paired with her real and heartfelt approach, made the book accessible to a wide spectrum of people, regardless of their familiarity with poetry.

Viral Success on Social Media

The success of "Milk and Honey" was further heightened by the power of social media. Readers who had followed Rupi on platforms like Instagram gladly embraced the opportunity to buy a physical copy of her work. They shared their pleasure and appreciation for the book on their own social media sites, leading to a viral spread of enthusiasm.

Social media influencers and celebrities also played a role in publicizing "Milk and Honey." Rupi's work resonated with a generation of readers who found her poetry to be both intensely personal and broadly relevant. Celebrities and prominent figures showed their praise for the book, further boosting its popularity.

"Milk and Honey" had a significant part in transforming Rupi Kaur from a budding poet and artist into a literary phenomenon. The book's popularity not only catapulted her work to a global audience but also spurred discussions about the changing face of writing in the digital age.

Rupi's journey from a teenage immigrant who published her poems on social media to a best-selling novelist exemplifies the democratization of literature. It shows how artists in the digital age may directly engage with their audience, avoiding traditional publishing gatekeepers. Her success motivated other writers to explore similar pathways to artistic expression and publication.

Analyzing "Milk and Honey"

Scholars and literary critics evaluated "Milk and Honey" in the light of current literature. They analyzed the book's unique combination of poetry and illustration and its impact on the growing landscape of poetry. The book's thematic examination of love, pain, healing, and self-discovery, seen through the lens of a young lady navigating the difficulties of modern life, resonated with many readers.

Rupi Kaur's minimalist and emotionally intense approach also provoked discussions regarding the developing notion of poetry. Her verses, frequently distinguished by brevity and clarity, were contrasted with more traditional types of poetry. This led to disputes regarding the importance of simplicity and accessibility in modern poetry and its capacity to reach new and diverse audiences.

International Bestseller and Literary Phenomenon

"Milk and Honey" became an international bestseller, reaching readers around the world. It was translated into multiple languages, making Rupi Kaur's work accessible to a global audience. The book's universal themes and the emotional depth of its substance crossed cultural boundaries, allowing readers from varied backgrounds to connect with its words.

Rupi Kaur's literary phenomenon was highlighted with book signings, speaking engagements, and appearances at literary festivals. She communicated with her readers personally, often providing personal tales and insights into her creative process. The book's significance expanded beyond the written word, influencing talks about the value of art and language in healing and self-discovery.

"Milk and Honey" represents a literary milestone in the life of Rupi Kaur. The creation and publishing of her first book represented a transformative event in her artistic journey. The book's acclaim, heightened by the power of social media and its themes of love, pain, healing, and self-discovery, rocketed Rupi Kaur to literary stardom.

It spurred discussions about the expanding landscape of literature and the ability of modern poetry to connect with varied worldwide audiences. The success of "Milk and Honey" acted as an inspiration for both budding artists and readers seeking accessible and real voices in the digital age.

Chapter 6

The Themes of Rupi Kaur's Poetry

One of the fundamental and frequent themes of Rupi Kaur's poems is love. Her verses cover numerous levels of love, from the intensity of romantic relationships to the strong link between family members. Rupi's poems portray the nuances of love, including its joys, tragedies, and transformative power.

In her poetry, love is typically portrayed as a power that can both raise and devastate. She digs into the emotions of longing, desire, and vulnerability that accompany love, giving light to the human experience of connection and attachment. Rupi's description of love is extremely intimate, often drawing from her own experiences and feelings.

The impact of this issue is significant, as it resonates with readers who have experienced the beauty and tribulations of love in their own lives. Rupi's ability to convey the essence of love in simple yet emotionally packed verses allows readers to connect with her work on a deeply intimate level.

Rupi Kaur's poetry is interwoven with themes of feminism and the empowerment of women. She addresses the feminine experience, looking into the problems, successes, and perseverance of women in a patriarchal culture. Her verses demonstrate her passion for subverting societal norms and opposing gender-based prejudice.

Rupi's poetry generally addresses subjects such as body positivity, self-acceptance, and the courage of women in the face of hardship. She celebrates the female body and its beauty, while also addressing the problems women experience in a world that often objectifies and commodifies them.

The impact of Rupi's feminist ideas is far-reaching. Her poetry has inspired numerous women to embrace their individuality, challenge cultural norms, and fight against gender inequity. Her work has contributed to significant discourses about feminism and has given voice to the experiences of many women.

Healing

Healing is a common theme in Rupi Kaur's poetry, tightly connected with her investigation of love and feminism. Her lyrics provide peace and hope to individuals who have faced grief, trauma, or heartbreak. Rupi's work often acts as a type of catharsis, both for herself and her audience.

She emphasizes the significance of self-care and self-love as key milestones on the journey to rehabilitation. Rupi's poetry expresses the concept that healing is a journey, one that may require accepting grief, embracing vulnerability, and finding strength in the process. Her remarks convey a sense of reassurance to individuals who are on their own healing journeys.

The impact of Rupi's healing theme is extremely personal for many readers. Her poetry has been a source of consolation and inspiration for many living with emotional scars, reminding them that they are not alone in their battles. Her work has played a vital influence in developing talks about mental health and emotional well-being.

Identity

Rupi Kaur's examination of identity is another major issue in her poems. She dives into the complexity of cultural identity, the immigrant experience, and the interplay of many identities. Her work depicts the dichotomy of her own identity as an Indian immigrant reared in Canada.

Rupi's poetry generally touches on the issue of belonging and the search for a sense of self in a world that sometimes demands conformity. She celebrates diversity and encourages readers to accept their unique identities, whether they are molded by ethnicity, culture, gender, or personal experiences.

The significance of Rupi's identity topic is far-reaching, as it connects with readers who deal with concerns of identity and belonging. Her work has provided a voice for those who traverse the intricacies of numerous identities and has contributed to discussions about cultural diversity and the significance of self-acceptance.

The Impact of These Themes

The impact of the recurring themes in Rupi Kaur's poetry is profound and multi-faceted. Her investigation of love has helped readers to connect with the common feelings linked with human relationships. Her feminist themes have empowered women and encouraged vital talks about gender equality.

Her focus on healing has brought comfort and support to many struggling with pain and trauma. Her investigation of identity has celebrated variety and encouraged self-acceptance.

Rupi's poetry serves as a strong reminder of the potential of words to heal, empower, and inspire. Her verses have connected with a varied global audience, and her work has crossed cultural and linguistic boundaries.

The impact of her topics extends beyond the pages of her books and the screens of social media, contributing to critical societal conversations and supporting positive change.

The Intersection of Themes

What makes Rupi Kaur's poetry particularly poignant is the junction of these subjects. Her investigation of love is connected with feminism, as she celebrates the strength and perseverance of women in the context of relationships. recovery and self-acceptance are strongly related, as her lines generally emphasize the necessity of self-love as a path to recovery.

Additionally, the notion of identity permeates all areas of her work, offering a framework for her investigation of love, feminism, and healing. The duality of her identity as an immigrant and a lady of Indian descent shapes her viewpoint and serves as a prism through which she observes the world.

The recurring themes of love, feminism, healing, and identity in Rupi Kaur's poetry have had a tremendous impact on her readers and society in general. Her ability to capture the core of these issues in simple yet emotionally packed lines has allowed her work to touch deeply with a varied global audience.

Through her writings, Rupi Kaur has empowered, inspired, and brought solace to individuals who have found meaning and connection in her poetry. Her writing continues to be a source of inspiration and a catalyst for crucial conversations in the world of literature and beyond.

Chapter 7

Social Activism

From the outset of her career, Rupi Kaur has shown a great devotion to social and political problems. Her advocacy activity spans a wide range of subjects, including feminism, gender equality, racial justice, and more. Rupi truly believes that art can be a powerful force for change, and she has utilized her platform to promote awareness and motivate action.

One of her earliest and most recognized areas of activism is feminism. Rupi has continually utilized her poems to protest gender-based prejudice and inequity. Her art generally tackles the perspectives and problems of women in a patriarchal culture. Rupi's fervent commitment to feminism has earned her distinction as a notable feminist poet, and she continues to be a powerful voice in the battle for gender equality.

Rupi has also been vocal about problems relating to diversity and representation in literature and the arts. She has stated her concerns about the lack of diversity in the publishing sector and the need for greater inclusivity. This campaign has prompted crucial conversations about representation and the hurdles that underrepresented voices often encounter.

Racial justice is another significant topic of interest for Rupi Kaur. As an artist of color, she is profoundly committed to raising awareness about racial inequalities and pushing for change. Her poetry generally examines the experiences of immigrants and the problems they confront, shining light on the complicated themes surrounding cultural identity and belonging.

Using Art as Activism

Rupi Kaur truly thinks that art can be a powerful form of activism. Her poetry serves as a method to educate, create awareness, and inspire social change. Through her art, she discusses major cultural topics and inspires her viewers to think about their own ideas and ideals.

One of the ways Rupi uses her art as activism is by expressing her personal experiences and emotions. Her poetry typically conveys the reality of love, heartbreak, healing, and self-discovery, creating a platform for readers to relate to their own feelings and experiences.

By revealing her personal weaknesses and problems, she invites others to do the same, creating a space for empathy and understanding.

Rupi's work typically questions cultural conventions and expectations, particularly when it comes to gender roles and stereotypes. Her feminist themes challenge engrained patriarchal notions and urge women to assert their identities and fight for equality. Rupi's poetry has been a source of empowerment for women worldwide, urging them to speak up against gender-based discrimination and campaign for their rights.

In addition to her poetry, Rupi employs visual art as a means of advocacy. Her paintings and visual compositions often complement her words, boosting their impact and adding another depth of meaning. These pictures can be thought-provoking and have a considerable influence on the understanding of her work.

Feminism and Gender Equality

Feminism and gender equality are major themes in Rupi Kaur's poetry and activism. Her work questions conventional gender stereotypes and shows the trials and successes of women in a patriarchal society. Through her art, she urges women to embrace their identities, defy societal norms, and speak up for their rights.

Rupi's poetry generally explores the topics of body positivity and self-acceptance, particularly in a world that often objectifies and commodifies women. Her words highlight the beauty of the female form and empower women to love and accept themselves as they are. By fostering self-confidence and self-worth, she adds to the greater discourse around self-image and body positivity.

Her thoughts on feminism extend beyond her work. Rupi Kaur is an outspoken champion of gender equality and women's rights. She uses her platform to raise awareness about gender-based discrimination and the need for societal change. Her advocacy entails speaking out against topics such as the gender pay gap, sexual harassment, and women's access to education and healthcare.

Rupi Kaur also emphasizes the necessity of intersectional feminism, acknowledging that the lives of women are affected by a complex interaction of elements, including race, ethnicity, sexuality, and financial background. She advocates for the inclusion and empowerment of all women, regardless of their background.

Racial Justice and Advocacy

As an artist of color, Rupi Kaur is profoundly committed to pushing for racial justice. Her poetry generally addresses the hardships of immigrants and the problems they face in a strange country. She stresses the complexity of cultural identification and belonging, shedding emphasis on the concerns of racial injustice and prejudice.

Rupi utilizes her poems to fight racial prejudices and promote diversity and inclusivity. She fights for the visibility of disadvantaged voices in literature and the arts, highlighting the significance of a more inclusive and fair cultural landscape.

In addition to her art, Rupi has actively participated in discussions and efforts linked to racial fairness. She has utilized her platform to promote the voices of other artists and activists calling for racial equality. Her advocacy extends to talks about structural racism, cultural appropriation, and the need for social and policy change.

Rupi Kaur's Global Impact

Rupi Kaur's impact as an activist stretches far beyond her poems and art. Her art has reached a global audience, prompting folks throughout the world to ponder on significant societal concerns.

Her ability to use art as a weapon for action has not only educated and raised awareness but also pushed others to engage in similar activities.

Her activism is marked by its accessibility and relatability. Rupi's poetry is intensely personal and emotionally charged, making it approachable to a wide spectrum of people. Her work has the capacity to connect with individuals on a personal level, promoting empathy and understanding.

Rupi's usage of social media has been essential in her advocacy. Her internet presence allows her to reach a broad audience and engage in vital debates about the themes and issues she covers in her work. She frequently participates in dialogues with her fans, replying to their queries and giving information relating to social and political causes.

Through her advocacy and art, Rupi Kaur has inspired her readers and fans to become more aware and engaged in societal concerns. Her work has given a source of inspiration for anyone trying to make a difference, whether via art, advocacy, or community involvement.

Rupi Kaur's commitment to social and political causes, particularly her advocacy for feminism, gender equality, and racial justice, has been a prominent feature of her work. Her belief in the power of art as a vehicle for action has allowed her to educate, inspire, and raise awareness about crucial societal concerns.

Her work, defined by its accessibility and relatability, has touched strongly with readers worldwide, generating empathy and understanding. Rupi's ability to utilize her art to challenge societal norms and promote change has encouraged others to engage in similar endeavors, making her a notable advocate and activist in the world of literature and beyond. Her work continues to serve as a source of inspiration and empowerment for individuals who aspire to have a positive effect on society.

Chapter 8

Rupi Kaur's Global Reach

Rupi Kaur's climb to international recognition has been nothing short of miraculous. Her journey from posting her poems on Instagram to becoming a widely famous poet and artist is a monument to the power of the digital era and the resonance of her work.

One of the primary causes behind Rupi's global success is the accessibility of her paintings. Her poetry, defined by its simplicity and emotional depth, transcends linguistic and cultural boundaries. Her use of social media, particularly Instagram, has allowed her to connect with readers from varied backgrounds and nations, building a global community of poetry fans.

Rupi's first novel, "Milk and Honey," acted as a trigger for her international popularity. The book, self-published and initially disseminated through her personal website and social media, connected emotionally with readers worldwide. Its themes of love, feminism, healing, and identity struck a chord with a varied audience, transcending boundaries and cultural barriers.

As "Milk and Honey" gained popularity, Rupi's work was translated into other languages, making it available to a global readership. Her art and topics resonated with folks from varied backgrounds, allowing them to connect with her poems on a personal level. The international popularity of "Milk and Honey" cleared the path for her future works and secured her reputation as a globally famous poet.

Rupi's influence extends beyond her poems and books. She has become a cultural figure, representing a new generation of poets who use social media as a forum for creative expression. Her impact on the world of literature, particularly in the digital age, has been tremendous, inspiring emerging poets to embrace new ways of sharing their work.

Stories of Individuals Touched by Rumi's Poetry

Rupi Kaur's poetry has impacted the lives of individuals across the globe, bringing solace, inspiration, and a sense of connection. Here are a few stories that highlight the depth of her impact:

1. Hina from Pakistan:

Hina, a young woman from Pakistan, found Rupi Kaur's poems through a friend's advice. She was immediately taken to the simplicity and emotional depth of Rupi's verses. As a woman living in a restrictive culture, Hina found courage and empowerment in Rupi's feminist themes. The poetry on self-acceptance and rejecting societal standards struck powerfully with her. Rupi's poems became a source of inspiration and a reminder that she could assert her identity and fight for gender equality, even in a community with ingrained norms.

2. Akio from Japan:

Akio, a college student from Japan, stumbled upon Rupi Kaur's Instagram account while searching for poetry online. The blend of poetry and visual art quickly grabbed him. Rupi's poems on love and healing helped him traverse the intricacies of relationships and personal growth.

He was moved by the simplicity and emotional depth of her work and began to explore poetry as a form of self-expression. Rupi's influence extended beyond his reading habits; it fueled his passion for poetry and art, pushing him to develop his own work.

3. Isabella from Brazil:

Isabella, a high school teacher from Brazil, introduced Rupi Kaur's poetry to her students as part of a creative writing assignment. The themes of love and identity resonated with her students, who found a voice in Rupi's remarks. Through analyzing and discussing Rupi's work, the students engaged in vital conversations about gender equality and self-acceptance. Rupi's poetry became a springboard for thought-provoking discussions and inspired a new generation of authors and activists.

4. Amir from Afghanistan:

Amir, a young man from Afghanistan, came upon Rupi Kaur's art while pursuing his education overseas. Her writings about ethnic identity and belonging struck a chord with him, as he wrestled with his own experiences as an immigrant. Rupi's examination of the immigrant experience provided him with a sense of validation and connection. Her words served as a reminder that he was not alone in his journey and that there were others who experienced similar problems.

5. Sofia from Spain:

Sofia, a writer from Spain, considered Rupi Kaur's poems to be a source of creative inspiration. Rupi's work motivated Sofia to examine her own feelings and experiences via writing. She appreciated Rupi's ability to portray complicated emotions in simple yet meaningful lyrics. Rupi's influence stretched beyond the pages of her novels; it spurred Sofia's creative path and emboldened her to share her own work with the world.

Rupi Kaur's global appeal is a testament to the universality and accessibility of her poetry. Her influence stretches far beyond her writings and social media presence, touching the lives of individuals from all origins and countries. The stories of individuals who have been deeply moved by her poems highlight the profound influence of her work and the sense of connection it creates.

Rupi's ability to use art as a platform for change has motivated others to embrace their identities, challenge conventional standards, and join in vital conversations about feminism, gender equality, and racial justice. Her influence has inspired a desire for poetry and creative expression in a new generation of authors and artists.

As a worldwide famous poet and campaigner, Rupi Kaur continues to serve as an inspiration for people striving to make a positive effect on the world. Her work reminds us of the transformational power of art and the ability of words to unite people across borders, countries, and languages.

Chapter 9

Challenges and Criticisms

Rupi Kaur's spectacular climb to prominence has not been without its fair share of critics and controversies. As a notable poet and artist, her work has drawn both ardent lovers and loud adversaries. These criticisms frequently concentrate on several fundamental characteristics of her work:

1. Simplicity & Minimalism:
One of the biggest complaints aimed against Rupi Kaur's poetry is its simplicity and brevity. Some literary critics claim that her writing lacks the depth and complexity generally associated with conventional poetry. They say that her minimalist approach, defined by brief, emotionally charged verses, lacks the richness and nuance of more classical poetry forms.

Critics have also questioned whether her work should be regarded as poetry, considering its unusual character. Some believe that it more closely resembles prose or aphorisms due to its brevity and directness.

2. Over-Exposure and Popularity:

Rupi Kaur's tremendous popularity, particularly on social media, has been both a blessing and a source of criticism. Some say that the enormous visibility of her work on platforms like Instagram has led to its over-saturation, lessening the sense of originality and intimacy that poetry frequently conveys.

Critics claim that the sheer amount of Kaur's posts, often accompanied by visually attractive pictures, can make her work feel more like commercial content than true artistic expression.

3. Lack of Complexity:

Another topic of dispute revolves around the perceived lack of complexity in her work. Some reviewers claim that her poems tend to address universal subjects in a relatively basic and uncomplicated manner. They imply that the emotional impact of her work may come at the sacrifice of subtlety and academic depth.

4. Self-Publication and Marketing:

The fact that Rupi Kaur initially self-published "Milk and Honey" and utilized her personal website and social media to promote her work has sparked questions about the impact of marketing and self-promotion in the literary world. Critics say that her success may be more a result of successful marketing methods and social media prowess than the inherent quality of her poetry.

5. Lack of Literary Prowess:

Some naysayers have critiqued Rupi Kaur's poetry for what they regard as a lack of literary prowess. They contend that her work does not display a grasp of classic poetry techniques and forms, such as meter, rhyme, and intricate metaphors. Critics have questioned whether her work should be subjected to the same standards as more conventional poetry.

Racial and Gender Criticisms

Rupi Kaur has also experienced criticisms relating to her identity as a woman of color and her exploration of feminist themes. Some say that her attention to these issues may have led to her popularity, while others contend that her work can be viewed as "trendy" due to its connection with contemporary social and political discussions.

These objections touch on problems of authenticity and whether Rupi's identity has been commodified for the purpose of her career.

Responses to Criticisms

Rupi Kaur has not been passive in the face of criticism. Her reactions to obstacles and conflicts have been marked by a commitment to maintaining her identity as a poet and artist. Here are some of the ways she has answered criticisms:

1. Embracing Simplicity:

Rather than shying away from her minimalist style, Rupi Kaur has embraced it. She regards her writing as accessible and relatable, allowing readers to relate to the feelings and events she portrays. She has underlined that poetry should not be bound to a single style or structure and that the brevity of her verses serves a purpose: to portray complex emotions clearly.

2. Remaining True to Her Vision:

Rupi Kaur has continuously kept true to her artistic vision and has not compromised her work to fit external expectations. She feels that poetry should be a representation of personal experiences and feelings. She continues to write about issues that are extremely meaningful to her, such as love, healing, feminism, and identity.

3. Fostering Dialogue:

Rather than avoiding criticism, Rupi Kaur has promoted interaction and open discussions about her work. She considers criticism as an opportunity for growth and contemplation. She constantly connects with her readers and detractors on social media, responding to inquiries and concerns. This open attitude allows her to preserve honesty and genuineness.

4. Expanding Literary Horizons:

Rupi Kaur has acknowledged the concerns regarding her work's simplicity and has actively worked to widen her literary horizons. She has introduced elements of storytelling and narrative into her more recent work, exploring diverse styles and subjects. This desire to evolve and explore displays her devotion to artistic growth and sincerity.

5. Engaging with Social Issues:

Rupi Kaur has not shied away from using her position to engage with social concerns and advocate change. She actively pushes for feminism, gender equality, and racial justice, attempting to use her work as a platform for activism and awareness. By tackling societal challenges through her art, she highlights the necessity of honest artistic expression and social influence.

Rupi Kaur's journey as a poet and artist has been marked by both acclaim and criticism. While her work may not correspond to traditional poetic rules, it has indisputably connected with a global audience, creating crucial discussions about poetry, art, and the power of words.

Rupi's replies to critiques have shown her devotion to sincerity and creative integrity. She remains steadfast in her vision and the issues that are meaningful to her, even as she continues to mature and broaden her literary horizons.

Criticism is an intrinsic part of the artistic journey, and Rupi Kaur's willingness to engage with it honestly and carefully underlines the depth of her commitment to her craft and her confidence in the power of art to connect with and inspire others on a personal level.

Chapter 10

Personal Life and Relationships

Rupi Kaur was born on October 4, 1992, in Hoshiarpur, Punjab, India. Her family immigrated to Canada when she was just four years old, seeking better prospects and a new life in a faraway nation. Rupi's early years were shaped by the experiences of being an immigrant, battling with cultural adaption, and the difficulty of negotiating a new identity.

Rupi's family played a crucial part in her life and development as a poet. Her parents, in particular, shaped her perspective on culture, identity, and heritage. The dichotomy of her identity as an Indian immigrant raised in Canada became a constant motif in her poetry.

As Rupi Kaur grew up, she watched the challenges and sacrifices her family made as immigrants. These experiences of cultural exile and the pursuit of the "Canadian dream" had a lasting mark on her and would eventually find expression in her poems.

Rupi's path as a poet began in her childhood. She discovered a love for art and expression at a young age, thanks in part to her mother, who exposed her to the world of drawing and painting. Rupi's early experiences with visual art established the groundwork for her future work as both a poet and a visual artist.

As a child, Rupi Kaur was contemplative and intimately attached to her emotions. She used painting as a tool to analyze her feelings and convey her thoughts. Her creativity was developed by her mother, who noticed and encouraged her artistic talents. The process of drawing and painting allowed Rupi to give voice to her emotions and engage with her inner world.

Rupi's family also played a key part in cultivating her love for reading and storytelling. Her parents filled their home with books and stories from their own cultural history, providing Rupi with a rich literary environment. The storylines she found in these books and the events she observed as an immigrant child would eventually become sources of inspiration for her work.

Educational Journey and the Discovery of Writing

Rupi Kaur's school journey substantially influenced her development as a writer. She attended the University of Waterloo in Ontario, Canada, where she studied rhetoric and professional writing. Her scholastic studies exposed her to the power of words and the art of storytelling, developing in her a strong passion for the written word.

It was during her time at university that Rupi discovered her affinity for writing. She began to dabble with poetry and prose, using her words to explore her personal experiences as an immigrant, a woman, and a member of the South Asian diaspora. The themes that would eventually saturate her writing, such as identity, love, feminism, and healing, were already taking shape during this formative period.

The supportive attitude of her academic environment motivated Rupi to share her work with others. She began performing at open mic events and meeting with fellow poets and writers, further fuelling her enthusiasm for creative expression. It was during these early phases of her writing journey that she discovered the power of her words to resonate with others.

The Influence of Relationships on Her Writing

Rupi Kaur's poetry generally draws from her personal experiences and relationships. Her verses are firmly entrenched in the emotions she has felt and the connections she has built with others. Her examination of love, heartbreak, healing, and self-identity is often motivated by her own encounters with these issues.

Rupi's work demonstrates a great awareness of the complexity of relationships. Her poems depict the joys and sufferings of love, capturing the feelings that accompany emotional connections. Her delicate lyrics address vulnerability, desire, and the intricacies of human connection. These issues are profoundly personal to her, and her writings resonate with readers who have experienced similar feelings in their own lives.

In her poems, Rupi Kaur also addresses the issue of healing, drawing from her own experiences of growth and self-discovery. Her work encourages readers to embrace self-care and self-love, principles she has learned from her own journey toward health. The honesty of her writing originates from her personal connection to these issues, making her poetry relevant and reassuring to individuals who have endured suffering and trauma.

Rupi's investigation of identity is rooted in her personal experiences as an immigrant and a woman of Indian descent. The dichotomy of her identity, influenced by her cultural heritage and her upbringing in Canada, affects her perspective on belonging and cultural diversity. Her personal connection to these subjects allows her to portray their nuances and resonates emotionally with readers who deal with questions of identity and self-acceptance.

The Impact of Relationships on Her Writing Style

Rupi Kaur's literary style is marked by its emotional intensity and simplicity. Her poems are frequently brief, expressing powerful themes with a minimalistic approach. This style is a reflection of her emotional connection to her work and her aim to portray complicated emotions in an approachable and understandable manner.

Rupi's experiences in relationships have impacted her lyrical style, allowing her to address highly intimate issues with directness and tenderness. Her poetry is an extension of her inner world, allowing readers to engage with her words on a deeply personal level. The simplicity of her poems serves the objective of making her poetry approachable and relatable, enabling readers to engage with their own feelings and experiences.

Rupi Kaur's personal life and relationships have played a key part in creating her identity as a poet and artist. Her experiences as an immigrant, her love for art and expression, her educational career, and her relationships have all inspired the themes and style of her work.

Rupi's poetry draws from her personal experiences, allowing her to portray complicated feelings with simplicity and emotional depth. Her work demonstrates her devotion to genuineness and her desire to connect with readers on a personal level. The impact of her experiences on her writing is a monument to the strength of personal connection and the ability of words to portray the depths of the human experience.

Chapter 11

The Future of Rupi Kaur

Rupi Kaur's journey as a poet and artist has been distinguished by continuous growth and evolution. While it's impossible to foresee the exact course of her career, we may offer some educated assumptions about what the future may bring for her:

1. Literary Exploration:
Rupi Kaur has exhibited an openness to literary research and innovation. Her earliest work was characterized by minimalist poetry, but she has now expanded her horizons to encompass longer narratives and storytelling. It is likely that she will continue to explore numerous literary genres and styles, giving readers fresh and diverse insights.

2. Activism and Advocacy:

Rupi's commitment to social and political problems is expected to remain a key feature in her future work. Her fight for feminism, gender equality, and racial justice will continue to impact her art. We may expect to see more poetry and art that addresses these concerns, stimulating crucial conversations and promoting awareness.

3. Global Engagement:

Given her international renown and global reach, Rupi Kaur's future works may combine themes and experiences from a diverse range of cultures and countries. Her poems and art have the ability to continue connecting with people from all backgrounds, generating a sense of oneness and global understanding.

4. Evolution of Identity:

As Rupi's own identity and experiences grow, so too will her writing. Her journey as an artist and as an individual is sure to bring fresh perspectives on themes of identity, cultural heritage, and personal growth. Her future works may reveal fresh layers of depth and contemplation.

5. Expanding Artistic Horizons:
Rupi Kaur's artistic talent extends beyond poetry, and we may anticipate witnessing a deeper study of visual art in her future works. Her blend of written words and graphic elements has already proven to be a potent medium for artistic expression. Her future endeavors may continue to push the frontiers of artistic forms.

6. Ongoing Digital Engagement:
Rupi Kaur's active connection with her readers on social media platforms is expected to endure. Her presence on Instagram, where she publishes her art and interacts with her audience, helps her to maintain a direct and personal connection with her fans. This digital participation will

certainly remain a crucial aspect of her profession.

The Ongoing Impact on Literature and Society

Rupi Kaur's influence on literature and culture is substantial and lasting. Her impact is likely to remain and expand in the following ways:

1. Inspiring Emerging Poets:

Rupi's success story has inspired a new generation of poets to explore the world of digital publishing and social networking. Her ability to connect with readers on a personal level and acquire global fame has cleared the road for other rising poets to express their work and creative vision.

2. Shaping Conversations:

Rupi Kaur's work has been significant in fostering important discourses about feminism, gender equality, racial justice, and cultural identity. Her poems and art continue to encourage discussions and awareness around these subjects, building a more inclusive and equal society.

3. Expanding the Definition of Poetry:
Rupi's simple style and accessible poetry have widened the definition of what constitutes poetry in the modern literary environment. Her popularity has spurred poets to embrace new styles and genres, breaking the traditional bounds of the discipline.

4. Global Community Building:
Rupi Kaur's writing has built a global community of readers who connect through similar experiences and emotions. This sense of connection and unity will likely continue to expand, boosting cross-cultural understanding and empathy.

In researching the life and work of Rupi Kaur, we have unearthed the incredible journey of a poet who has resonated with people around the world. Her personal experiences as an immigrant, her love for art and expression, her scholastic career, and her relationships have all inspired the themes and style of her poetry.

As we hypothesize about the future of Rupi Kaur, we see a poet and artist committed to growth, experimentation, and activism. Her work will certainly continue to expand and address major societal challenges. Her global impact on literature and society is a tribute to the ability of art to connect people on a personal level and inspire positive change.

Rupi Kaur's legacy is one of empowerment, sincerity, and devotion to using art as a means of connecting with the human experience. Her path as a poet is ongoing, and her influence on the world of poetry and beyond will likely continue to resound with generations to come